A ROOKIE READER®

CONSTANCE STUMBLES

By Patricia and Fredrick McKissack

Illustrations by Tom Dunnington

Prepared under the direction of Robert Hillerich, Ph.D.

CHILDRENS PRESS®

CHICAGO

LIBRARY OF CONGRESS
Library of Congress Cataloging-in-Publication Data

McKissack, Pat, 1944-
    Constance stumbles / by Pat & Fredrick McKissack ;
Tom Dunnington, illustrator.
      p. cm. — (A Rookie Reader)
    Summary: Despite many setbacks, a little girl is
determined to learn to ride a bicycle.
    ISBN 0-516-02086-2
    [1. Bicycles and bicycling—Fiction.] I. McKissack,
Fredrick. II. Dunnington, Tom, ill. III. Title. IV. Series.
PZ7.M478693Co 1988
[E]—dc19   87-33782
                                         CIP
                                         AC

Childrens Press®, Chicago
Copyright © 1988 by Regensteiner Publishing Enterprises, Inc.
All rights reserved. Published simultaneously in Canada.
Printed in the United States of America.
 2 3 4 5 6 7 8 9 10 R 97 96 95 94 93 92 91 90 89

Watch out, Constance Stumbles.

OOPS!

Take your time, Constance Stumbles.

UMPH!

Not now, Constance Stumbles.

7

ZIP!

Don't do it, Constance Stumbles.

YUK!

Be careful, Constance Stumbles.

OH!

Wait a minute, Constance Stumbles.

WHEE!

Look out, Constance Stumbles.

OUCH!

Too late, Constance Stumbles.

EEK!

Look up, Constance Stumbles.

AH!

Try it again, Constance Stumbles.

WHOA!

Not yet, Constance Stumbles.

YIP!

Hold on, Constance Stumbles.

OOOOOH!

Keep trying, Constance Stumbles.

UGH!

You did it, Constance Stumbles.

HOORAY!

WORD LIST

a	hooray	out	up
again	it	not	watch
be	keep	now	wait
careful	late	Stumbles	yet
Constance	look	take	you
did	minute	time	your
don't	oh	too	
do	on	try	
hold	ouch	trying	

WORD SOUNDS

ah	oops	whee	yuk
eek	ugh	whoa	zip
oooooh	umph	yip	

About the Authors

Patricia and **Fredrick McKissack** are free-lance writers, editors, and teachers of writing. They are the owners of All-Writing Services, located in Clayton, Missouri. Since 1975, the McKissacks have published numerous magazine articles and stories for juvenile and adult readers. They also have conducted educational and editorial workshops throughout the country. The McKissacks and their three teenage sons live in a large remodeled inner-city home in St. Louis.

About the Artist

Tom Dunnington hails from the Midwest, having lived in Minnesota, Iowa, Illinois, and Indiana. He attended the John Herron Institute of Art in Indianapolis and the American Academy of Art and the Chicago Art Institute in Chicago. He has been an art instructor and illustrator for many years. In addition to illustrating books, Mr. Dunnington is working on a series of paintings of endangered birds (produced as limited edition prints). His current residence is in Oak Park, Illinois, where he works as a free-lance illustrator and is active in church and community youth work.